Geography Shapes Our World

by Stephanie Sigue

Editorial Offices: Glenview, Illinois • Parsippany, New Jersey • New York, New York
Sales Offices: Needham, Massachusetts • Duluth, Georgia • Glenview, Illinois
Coppell, Texas • Ontario, California • Mesa, Arizona

ISBN: 0-328-13435-9

1 2 3 4 5 6 7 8 9 10 V0G1 14 13 12 11 10 09 08 07 06 05

Geography Shapes Culture

Imagine living by the ocean in Portugal. The ocean supplies your family with lots of fish to sell and to eat. But if you live in the grassy plains of Uruguay in South America, your family may raise cattle. And if you live in the city of Paris, you don't have to depend on what grows in the area. Food is shipped in from all over the world. Where you live has a lot to do with *how* you live.

The Earth is made up of seven different **continents**, connected by the Pacific, the Atlantic, the Indian and the Arctic Oceans. The continents are Asia, Africa, North America, South America, Antarctica, Europe, and Australia. Each continent has a different **climate** and **geography** and **industry**. Let's take a look at a few!

You can find maps like this in an atlas. An atlas provides information about the world.

3

Waking Up in Mali

"Wake up, Aminata!" calls her mother. Aminata wakes to another warm, **humid** day in Mali. She squats on the floor with her family and has a delicious breakfast of maize porridge. The maize is a kind of corn, which her family grows in a small plot of land just behind their house.

After eating, Aminata helps her mother sweep and wash dishes. By eight, her parents leave to work in the nearby cotton fields. Part of the money they make pays for Aminata's schooling.

Today at school, they are studying the Dogon people. The Dogon used to live high in the cliffs, in protective dwellings made of pink sandstone. They now live in the villages because life is easier, and they are closer to the Niger River.

Mali is the largest country in West Africa.

ATLANTIC OCEAN

WESTERN SAHARA

MALI

SENEGAL

GAMBIA

GUINEA-BISSAU

GUINEA

SIERRA LEONE

ATLANTIC OCEAN

MEDITERRANEAN SEA

Strait of Gibraltar

MOROCCO

TUNISIA

ALGERIA

LIBYA

SAHARA DESERT

MALI

NIGER

NIA

Niger

Bamako

BURKINA FASO

BENIN

Niger

Lake Chad

NIGERIA

IVORY COAST

TOGO

GHANA

CAMEROON

EQUATORIAL GUINEA

GABON

CONGO

5

The 21-string Kora

Aminata knows how important the Niger river is. Without it, how would her family **irrigate** crops? How would they travel to visit relatives?

When Aminata gets home, she helps her mother prepare the *poulet yassa,* which is the grilled perch that her father caught in the Niger.

After dinner, Aminata's father plays the *kora*, a instrument of 21 strings. It's made of rosewood which is found in Mali. The government prizes this music because it is **native**. Her uncle plays the drums. "Drums used to be played by people to send messages across the land," her uncle tells her.

That night, in her bed, Aminata listens to the crickets outside. Everything here seems to have a beat, and like the drums, she wonders what messages the crickets are repeating to one another.

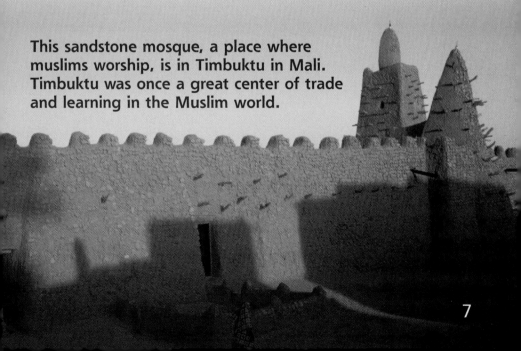

This sandstone mosque, a place where muslims worship, is in Timbuktu in Mali. Timbuktu was once a great center of trade and learning in the Muslim world.

Maria in Brazil

Maria wakes to beeping cars and loud conversations. Two out of three Brazilians live in a city, including Maria and her family, who live in São Paulo. Maria gets ready for school. She's luckier than Aminata because her schooling is free.

Brazil is close to the equator. From December to February it's summer, which is just one month away, and Maria can't wait! It's so hot that most people take vacation and school is then closed. Maria and her family will go to the beach and to the five-day Carnival, which is celebrated all over Brazil.

Today at school, Maria learns about the Amazon, the largest river in the world. Many people fish here and hunt along its banks.

São Paulo, the biggest city in South America.

São Paulo•

South America is the 4th largest continent in the world.

In the evening, Maria and her family eat rice, beans and fish that her father caught. Brazil is famous for coffee and all the adults drink it throughout the meal.

After dinner, Maria practices a little *repitismo* with her mother. It is a kind of call and response singing. "It's like a conversation," Maria's mother tells her. "In Brazil, music is the way to have a social gathering of family and friends. This is very important, especially in the rocky, arid areas where there aren't a lot of people."

By the time Maria goes to sleep, she is very tired. She thinks of what her mother told her about how important family and music are. She's glad she has her music and her family around her.

Brazilians eat the foods they grow locally. A typical Brazilian meal is arroz, or white rice, and black beans and fish.

Tampa

ATLANTIC OCEAN

FLORIDA

Miami

GULF OF MEXICO

Straits of Florida

Grand Bahama Ba...

Nassau

BAHA...
ISLAN...

Havana

CUBA

G R E A T E R

CAYMAN ISLANDS

Montego Bay

Kingston

JAMAICA

Jamaica is the largest of the English speaking islands. It is part of a group of islands called the Greater Antilles.

Marley in Jamaica

By the time Marley wakes up In Jamaica, it's already hot. Jamaica is in the Carribean so the weather is hot most of the year. It's a good thing you can cool off on so many of Jamaica's white sandy beaches!

Marley's parents are getting ready to work on the sugar **plantation**. Marley loves sugar cane because it flavors his favorite breakfast drink, hot cocoa. Cocoa is made from locally grown cacao beans.

Marley's parents prefer to drink coffee. Jamaica is full of mountains, including the huge Blue Mountains. Here the mists create the perfect soil and climate for growing coffee. Blue Mountain coffee is famous all over the world. It's no wonder Marley's parents love it.

HAITI DOMINICAN REPUBLIC PUERTO RICO

au-Prince

Santo Domingo

San Juan

T I L L E S

CARIBBEAN SEA

Marley in Jamaica

Marley is named after Bob Marley, one of the most famous musicians in Jamaica. Reggae is a free-spirited, spiritual music that Bob Marley made famous. Marley plays the guitar, just like his namesake. "The land inspires my music to be loud and bright," say many musicians, and Marley understands why. Jamaica is full of colorful flowers, bright blue sky and many friendly people.

Marley is lucky because he goes to school. Many children in Jamaica don't. Sometimes in late fall, he doesn't go to school because it's hurricane season. The weather is too fierce then.

Bob Marley and his band The Wailers popularized Reggae music.

At school, Marley is studying the rivers of Jamaica. There are over 120 of them! Is it any wonder so many people here love to go rafting?

School gets out at one o'clock so children can help their parents. Marley's job is to help tend the sweet potato crops in the small plot in his backyard.

At dinner, Marley and his family eat cowcod soup, which is made from bananas and yams. There is also jerk chicken which is chicken marinated in spices and fried. They also have sweet potatoes that Marley dug from their garden. At bedtime, Marley lays in bed and looks out at the night. There is a cooling offshore breeze coming in the window. Jamaicans call it "the doctor breeze" because it makes you feel better. Even the breeze, Marley thinks, has music in it.

Jamaican children love to play soccer.

Miko in Japan

The delicious smell of miso soup wakes Miko. Miso is made of fermented soybeans, which are one of Japan's natural **products**. Miko gets up from the straw mat where she sleeps. Japan is very humid, but these mats keep the floor cool now, and they will keep the floor warm in winter.

After Miko eats, she heads outside to school. The cherry blossoms are in bloom! Japan has more kinds of cherry trees than any other place on Earth, and when they bloom in April, everyone celebrates. The blossoms mean new beginnings. That's why the school and business years begin at this time. Later that evening, Miko and her family will go to the park to see the blossoms. Lots of other families will also be there. Miko's mother pickles the blossoms and makes a delicious hot drink from them.

In Japan, the roads are so crowded that many people find it easier to bicycle to work or to do the daily shopping.

CHINA

RUSSIA

Sappor

SEA OF
JAPAN

Korea Strait

JAPAN

Mt. Fuji

Toky

Kyoto

Osaka

PACIFIC
OCEAN

At school, they are learning about Japan's geography. Miko knows that there are many volcanoes and earthquakes which cause damage, but the country has learned to track them. Miko's school was even built to be quake resistant.

When Miko comes home for dinner, she takes off her shoes and puts on soft slippers. For dinner they are having sushi, which is raw fish and rice wrapped in seaweed. They will also have tempura, which is fish and vegetables fried in batter.

The family talks about what they will do in the fall. "We'll go see *Kagura*," Miko's father says. The dancers in this ceremony wear fancy costumes and masks. Kagura was originally a way to ask for good harvest.

Japan has several thousand islands. Most of Japan is mountains and hills, so people tend to live in crowded cities along the coastlines.

At night, Miko practices the *sanshin*, a kind of banjo. Her grandfather helps her because he wants to pass down the music traditions. He tells her that in Okinawa, where he once lived, the workers used to take their instruments right into the rice fields. "After work was done, we would play," he said. "It made working so much easier!"

Miko has seen a picture of her grandfather's house in Okinawa, where he lived before coming to live with them. It is surrounded by heavy stone walls. These protected his house from Japan's frequent **typhoons**.

Finally, Miko lays down on her mat to sleep. The scent of the cherry blossoms comes in through the window and lulls her to sleep.

The sanshin is a traditional three string banjo.

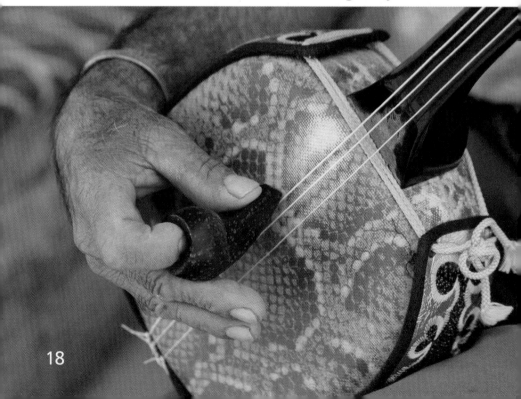

Gina Introduces Us to Rome

"Honk! Honk!" A car horn blasts and Gina's eyes fly open. She wakes up in one of the most famous cities in the world, Rome, Italy.

Gina lives in a modern apartment with her parents and her grandparents. Everyone has breakfast together, eating eggs and toast and cereal. On her way to school Gina dodges the honk of scooters and the rush of people coming and going.

Gina loves the city. You can walk just about anywhere, from the Forum to the Spanish Steps. Her favorite place is by the Coliseum, which is thousands of years old. And right on the same block as the Coliseum is a brand new store selling fancy shoes. There is a great sense of history here and also a sense of modern life. Living in Rome, Gina can't help but appreciate her past and her present.

These are the ancient ruins of the Temple of Saturn and the Arch of Severus in Rome.

19

Italy is a warm and sunny peninsula in southern Europe, extending into the Mediterranean Sea.

20

In school, Gina is learning about the dance *Tarantella*, which means spider. The dance began long ago as a cure for the spider bite. Dancers spun around wildly and danced away the poison!

At dinner that night, Gina's mother makes homemade pasta and sauce, which she calls gravy. They dip bread in olive oil that is made locally.

After dinner, Gina's father gives Gina a music lesson. She is learning to play the *organetti*, which is Italy's accordion. "Did you know the Italians invented the way we set down musical notes?" he asks. "That was the beginning of 'do re mi'."

Gina is so excited by her grandfather's stories she can hardly go to sleep. Her mind is as busy as Rome, the city she calls home.

Now Try This

You've read about a few of the countries of West Africa, Western Europe, South America, Asia, and the Caribbean and about some children who live in them. What do you think your life might be like if you lived in one of those countries? You can write a diary page to tell what your life is like in one of those countries.

1. Use an atlas. Turn to the maps of Africa, Europe, South America, Asia, or the Caribbean, and decide where you might like to live.

2. After you have chosen a country, use at least two resources, such as the Internet and books from the library, to find out more about it.

3. Think about living in one of those countries. Write a diary page about your day. What is the geography of your country like? What happens when you wake up? What happens in school? Is the weather hot or cold? What do you eat for breakfast? What sights do you see during your busy day?

4. Be sure to include some interesting facts in your report. Don't forget to tell what people do for fun. Make your report thorough and lively.

5. Add visuals to help describe the country.

6. Present your report to the group.

Glossary

climate *n.* the usual weather in a place

continents *n.* seven large land masses of the earth (Asia, Africa, Europe, North America, South America, Australia, and Antarctica)

geography *n.* the study of the earth, including its people, resources, climate, and physical features

industry *n.* manufacturing companies and other businesses

irrigate *v.* to supply water to crops by artificial means, such as channels and pipes

native *n.* a person , an animal, or a plant that originally lived or grew in a certain place

plantation *n.* a large farm found in warm climates where crops such as coffee, tea, rubber, and cotton are grown

product *n.* something that is manufactured or made by a natural process

typhoon *n.* a violent tropical storm